WITHDRAWN

Addition
Made Easy

Rebecca Wingard-Nelson

Enslow Elementary

an imprint of

Enslow Publishers, Inc.

40 Industrial Road   PO Box 38
Box 398   Aldershot
Berkeley Heights, NJ 07922   Hants GU12 6BP
      UK

Enslow Elementary, an imprint of Enslow Publishers, Inc.

Enslow Elementary® is a registered trademark of Enslow Publishers, Inc.

Library of Congress Cataloging-in-Publication Data

Wingard-Nelson, Rebecca.
    Addition made easy / Rebecca Wingard-Nelson.
        p. cm. — (Making math easy)
    Includes index.
    ISBN 0-7660-2508-X (hardcover)
    1. Addition—Juvenile literature. I. Title.
    QA115.W75 2005
    513.2'11—dc22

                                                2004021657

Printed in the United States of America

10 9 8 7 6 5 4 3

To Our Readers: We have done our best to make sure all Internet Addresses in this book were active and appropriate when we went to press. However, the author and the publisher have no control over and assume no liability for the material available on those Internet sites or on other Web sites they may link to. Any comments or suggestions can be sent by e-mail to comments@enslow.com or to the address on the back cover.

Illustrations: Tom LaBaff

Cover illustration: Tom LaBaff

Contents

Introduction

Math is all around, and an important part of anyone's life. You use math when you're playing games, cooking food, spending money, telling time, reading music, or doing any other activity that uses numbers. Even finding a television channel uses math!

Addition Is Everywhere

Every day you use addition, and you might not even know it. When you have one sticker, and your friend gives you one more sticker, you know that you have two stickers. Addition is that simple.

Using This Book

This book can be used to learn or review addition at your own speed. It can be used on your own or with a friend, tutor, or parent. Get ready to discover math . . . made easy!

Numbers and

Numbers are written using the following ten symbols, called digits.

$$0, 1, 2, 3, 4, 5, 6, 7, 8, 9$$

Numbers zero through nine are written using only one digit. Larger numbers are written using two or more digits.

The number 346 has three digits, each in a different place. Each place has a name that tells its value.

There is a 3 in the hundreds place.

3 HUNDREDS
4 TENS
6 ONES

Place Value

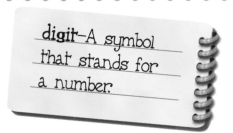

digit–A symbol that stands for a number.

In the number 346, the digit **6** is in the ones place. That means the digit has a value of 6 ones.

The digit **4** is in the tens place. It has a value of 4 tens.

The digit **3** is in the hundreds place. It has a value of 3 hundreds.

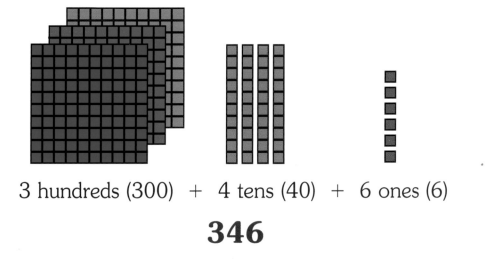

3 hundreds (300) + 4 tens (40) + 6 ones (6)

346

Adding One-

The one-digit numbers are

0, 1, 2, 3, 4, 5, 6, 7, 8, and 9.

When you add two numbers together, you find how many you have in all. If you have one soccer ball and add two soccer balls, you have three soccer balls in all.

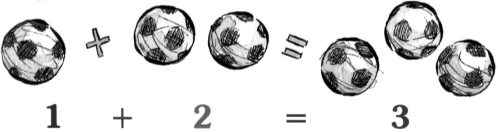

1   +   2   =   3

Let's try another one. If you have four blue marbles and then get two more red marbles, you have six marbles in all.

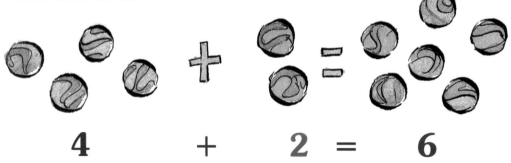

4   +   2   =   6

Digit Numbers

All of these equations have one-digit answers.

$0 + 0 = 0$	$2 + 2 = 4$	$4 + 3 = 7$
$0 + 1 = 1$	$2 + 4 = 6$	$4 + 4 = 8$
$0 + 3 = 3$	$2 + 5 = 7$	$5 + 0 = 5$
$0 + 4 = 4$	$2 + 7 = 9$	$5 + 1 = 6$
$0 + 7 = 7$	$3 + 1 = 4$	$5 + 3 = 8$
$1 + 1 = 2$	$3 + 3 = 6$	$5 + 4 = 9$
$1 + 3 = 4$	$3 + 4 = 7$	$6 + 0 = 6$
$1 + 4 = 5$	$3 + 5 = 8$	$6 + 2 = 8$
$1 + 6 = 7$	$3 + 6 = 9$	$7 + 2 = 9$
$2 + 0 = 2$	$4 + 0 = 4$	$8 + 1 = 9$

When you learn how to add one-digit numbers, adding larger numbers is easy.

Addition

Addition problems can be written two ways, in a line or in a column.

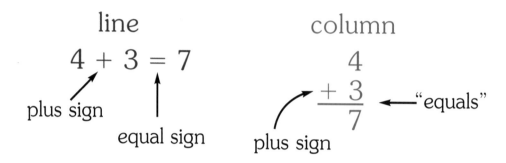

line

4 + 3 = 7

plus sign

equal sign

column

4
+ 3
7

"equals"

plus sign

When you read an addition problem out loud, you say,

4 + 3 = 7

Four plus three equals seven.

Terms

Numbers that are being added are called addends.

$$
\begin{array}{r}
6 \\
+\ 3 \\
\hline
9
\end{array}
$$

6 ← addend
+ 3 ← addend

The answer to an addition problem is called the sum.

$$
\begin{array}{r}
1 \\
+\ 4 \\
\hline
5
\end{array}
$$

5 ← sum

One plus four?

Five.

Column

You can add three or more numbers. Put the numbers under each other in a column. This is called column addtion.

$$1 + 4 + 2$$

Write the numbers in a column.

$$\begin{array}{r} 1 \\ 4 \\ + 2 \\ \hline \end{array}$$

Add any two of the numbers.

$$\begin{array}{r} 1 \\ 4 \\ + 2 \\ \hline \end{array} \quad 1 + 4 = 5$$

Now add the third number to the sum you just found.

$$\begin{array}{r} 1 \\ 4 \\ + 2 \\ \hline 7 \end{array} \quad 5 \quad 5 + 2 = 7$$

The sum of $1 + 4 + 2$ is 7.

Addition

In column addition, just keep adding numbers. When there are no more numbers to add, you are done! Look at another example.

3 + 2 + 3

Write the numbers in a column.

$$
\begin{array}{r}
3 \\
2 \\
+\ 3 \\
\hline
8
\end{array}
$$

Add two of the numbers.
$3 + 2 = 5$

Add the third number.
$5 + 3 = 8$

What Is

When you add numbers, sometimes the answer is more than 9. You can regroup! Regrouping changes a group of 10 ones into 1 ten.

10 ones   =   1 ten

Let's look at **6 + 6.**

6 ones + 6 ones   =   12 ones

The sum of 12 ones can be regrouped as 1 group of ten with 2 ones left over.

=

tens ones
1 2

The number 12 has a 1 in the tens place and a 2 in the ones place.

Regrouping?

7 + 8

tens · ones

```
    7
  + 8
 ‾‾‾‾
   15
```

7 ones + 8 ones = 15 ones

You can't write 15 ones in the ones place. There is only room for one digit in the ones place.

Regroup 15 ones as 1 ten and 5 ones. Write a 5 in the ones place. Write the 1 in the tens place.

In column addition, always add from right to left.

9 + 1

tens · ones

```
    9
  + 1
 ‾‾‾‾
   10
```

9 ones + 1 one = 10 ones

Regroup 10 ones as 1 ten and 0 ones. There are no ones! The number 0 is used as a placeholder to show that there are no ones after regrouping. Write the 0 in the ones place. Write the 1 in the tens place.

The Zero

The number zero means "nothing" or "none." Any number plus zero (0) equals the number. This is called the zero property of addition.

If you have five pigs and you get zero more (none), you still have five pigs.

$$5 + 0 = 5$$

If you start with zero pigs (none) and get five, you have five pigs.

$$0 + 5 = 5$$

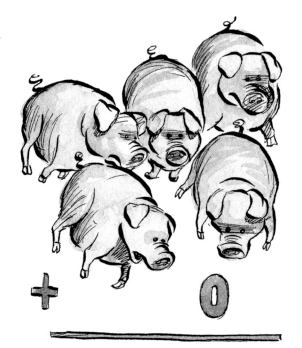

— we're still here!

Property

The zero property of addition is always true, no matter how large the number is that you are adding with zero.

$$\begin{array}{r} 1 \\ +\ 0 \\ \hline 1 \end{array} \qquad \begin{array}{r} 0 \\ +\ 9 \\ \hline 9 \end{array} \qquad \begin{array}{r} 12 \\ +\ 0 \\ \hline 12 \end{array}$$

$$\begin{array}{r} 0 \\ +\ 26 \\ \hline 26 \end{array} \qquad \begin{array}{r} 99 \\ +\ 0 \\ \hline 99 \end{array} \qquad \begin{array}{r} 102 \\ +\ 0 \\ \hline 102 \end{array}$$

$$\begin{array}{r} 891 \\ +\ 0 \\ \hline 891 \end{array} \qquad \begin{array}{r} 0 \\ +\ 1{,}243 \\ \hline 1{,}243 \end{array} \qquad \begin{array}{r} 1{,}204{,}612 \\ +\ 0 \\ \hline 1{,}204{,}612 \end{array}$$

The Commutative

You can use the same numbers to make different addition problems. Let's try the numbers 4 and 5.

$$4 + 5 = 9 \qquad 5 + 4 = 9$$

When the numbers being added change places, the answer stays the same. This is called the commutative property of addition.

You can remember the name of the property by knowing that when you commute, you to go back and forth, or change places.

Let's look at another one.

$$7 + 6 = 13$$
$$6 + 7 = 13$$

The sums are the same.

Property

When you know the sum of 3 + 4, you also know the sum of 4 + 3.

$$3 + 4 = 7 \qquad 4 + 3 = 7$$

The commutative property of addition is always true, no matter what numbers you are adding.

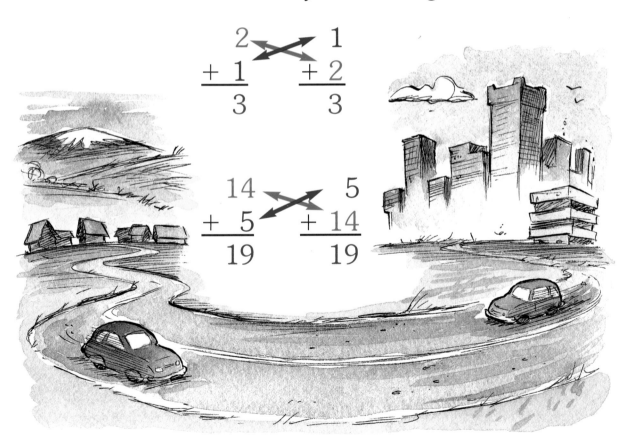

$$\begin{array}{r} 2 \\ + 1 \\ \hline 3 \end{array} \qquad \begin{array}{r} 1 \\ + 2 \\ \hline 3 \end{array}$$

$$\begin{array}{r} 14 \\ + 5 \\ \hline 19 \end{array} \qquad \begin{array}{r} 5 \\ + 14 \\ \hline 19 \end{array}$$

The Associative

Sometimes you need to add three or more numbers. You can use parentheses to show which two numbers get added first.

$$1 + 2 + 4$$

$(1 + 2) + 4$ says that 1 and 2 are added first.

Add inside the parentheses.

$$(1 + 2) + 4$$

$$\downarrow$$

$$3$$

Now add the third number.

$$3 + 4 = 7$$

$$\text{So, } (1 + 2) + 4 = 7$$

Watch what happens when the parentheses are put around a different set of numbers in the same problem.

Property

The Associative Property—
When adding three or more numbers, the way you group, or associate, the numbers does not change the answer.

$1 + (2 + 4)$ says that 2 and 4 are added first.

Add inside the parentheses.

$$1 + (2 + 4)$$

$$6$$

Now add the third number.

$$1 + 6 = 7$$

So, $1 + (2 + 4) = 7$

The answer did not change when the numbers were grouped in a different way. This is called the associative property of addition.

You can remember the associative property by knowing that associates are partners. In addition, you can associate or partner the numbers together in any way you choose.

Adding Two-

Write two-digit addition problems in columns. Line up the numbers so that the same place values are in the same column.

13 + 24

tens ones

```
  13    13 is the same as 1 ten and 3 ones
+ 24    24 is the same as 2 tens and 4 ones
```

13   1 ten   3

24   2 tens   4

Always add from right to left. First, add the numbers in the ones column. Write the answer in the ones place.

```
  13
+ 24        3 + 4 = 7
   7
```

Digit Numbers

Add the numbers in the tens column. Write the answer in the tens place.

$$\begin{array}{r} 13 \\ +\ 24 \\ \hline 37 \end{array}$$

$1 + 2 = 3$

Let's look at another one.

42 + 36

$$\begin{array}{r} 42 \\ +\ 36 \\ \hline \end{array}$$

Add the ones.

$$\begin{array}{r} 42 \\ +\ 36 \\ \hline 8 \end{array}$$

Add the tens.

$$\begin{array}{r} 42 \\ +\ 36 \\ \hline 78 \end{array}$$

Regrouping

Sometimes when you add two-digit numbers, the sum of the digits in the ones column is more than nine. Then what do you do?

18 + 5

$$\begin{array}{r} 18 \\ +5 \\ \hline 3 \end{array}$$

Add the numbers in the ones column. $8 + 5 = 13$. Regroup 13. 13 is the same as 1 ten and 3 ones. Write the 3 ones in the ones place.

$$\begin{array}{r} 1 \\ 18 \\ +5 \\ \hline 3 \end{array}$$

Carry the 1 to the tens column.

carry—To put a regrouped number into the next larger place-value column.

$$\begin{array}{r} 1 \\ 18 \\ +5 \\ \hline 23 \end{array}$$

Add the numbers in the tens column. Remember to include the number you carried. $1 + 1 = 2$. Write the 2 in the tens place.

and Carrying

Let's look at a problem that adds two two-digit numbers.

35 + 57

$$\begin{array}{r} 1 \\ 35 \\ + 57 \\ \hline 2 \end{array}$$

Add the numbers in the ones column. 5 + 7 = 12. Write the 2 ones in the ones place. Carry the 1 to the tens column.

$$\begin{array}{r} 1 \\ 35 \\ + 57 \\ \hline 92 \end{array}$$

Add the numbers in the tens column. Remember to include the number you carried from the ones place. There are now three digits to add in the tens column. 1 + 3 + 5 = 9. Write the 9 in the tens place.

Adding Three-

Adding three-digit numbers is just like adding two-digit numbers.

341 + 126

$$
\begin{array}{r}
341 \\
+\ 126 \\
\hline
\end{array}
$$

Write the numbers in columns. Line up the place values.

Always add from right to left.

$$
\begin{array}{r}
341 \\
+\ 126 \\
\hline
7
\end{array}
$$

Add the numbers in the ones column. $1 + 6 = 7$. Write the 7 in the ones place.

$$
\begin{array}{r}
341 \\
+\ 126 \\
\hline
67
\end{array}
$$

Add the numbers in the tens column. $4 + 2 = 6$. Write the 6 in the tens place.

$$
\begin{array}{r}
341 \\
+\ 126 \\
\hline
467
\end{array}
$$

Add the numbers in the hundreds column. $3 + 1 = 4$. Write the 4 in the hundreds place.

Digit Numbers

Let's look at a few more.

295	295	295	295
+ 503	+ 503	+ 503	+ 503
	8	98	798

654	654	654	654
+ 34	+ 34	+ 34	+ 34
	8	88	688

You don't scare me.
Your sum is 875.
HA!

Regrouping for

You can regroup numbers in any place value.

hundreds tens ones
4 9 6

Let's look at regrouping in the tens place.

496 + 213

```
  496
+ 213
```
Write the numbers in columns.
Line up the place values.

```
  496
+ 213
    9
```
Add the numbers in the ones column.
6 + 3 = 9. Write the 9 in the ones place.

```
   1
  496
+ 213
   09
```
Add the numbers in the tens column.
9 + 1 = 10. Regroup 10. 10 tens is is the same as 1 hundred. Write the 0 in the tens place. Carry the 1 to the hundreds column.

Three Digits

$$\begin{array}{r} 1 \\ 496 \\ + 213 \\ \hline 709 \end{array}$$

Add the numbers in the hundreds column. $1 + 4 + 2 = 7$. Write the 7 in the hundreds place.

ALL RIGHT TROOPS! LET'S REGROUP. HUSTLE! HUSTLE! HUSTLE!

When the sum of the numbers in the hundreds column is more than 9, regroup the hundreds as thousands. In the example below, write a 0 in the hundreds place, and write the 1 in the thousands place.

$$\begin{array}{r} 317 \\ + 730 \\ \hline \end{array} \qquad \begin{array}{r} 317 \\ + 730 \\ \hline 7 \end{array} \qquad \begin{array}{r} 317 \\ + 730 \\ \hline 47 \end{array} \qquad \begin{array}{r} 1 \\ 317 \\ + 730 \\ \hline 1{,}047 \end{array}$$

Adding Greater

Numbers that have more than three digits are added the same way as smaller numbers.

6,378 + 4,541

$$\begin{array}{r} 6,378 \\ +\ 4,541 \\ \hline \end{array}$$

Write the numbers in columns. Line up the place values.

$$\begin{array}{r} 6,378 \\ +\ 4,541 \\ \hline 9 \end{array}$$

Add the numbers in the ones column. 8 + 1 = 9. Write the 9 in the ones place.

$$\begin{array}{r} 1 \\ 6,378 \\ +\ 4,541 \\ \hline 19 \end{array}$$

Add the numbers in the tens column. 7 + 4 = 11. Regroup 11. 11 tens is the same as 1 hundred and 1 ten. Write the 1 in the tens place. Carry the 1 to the hundreds column.

$$\begin{array}{r} 1 \\ 6,378 \\ +\ 4,541 \\ \hline 919 \end{array}$$

Add the numbers in the hundreds column. 1 + 3 + 5 = 9 Write the 9 in the hundreds place.

Numbers

$$\begin{array}{r} {\scriptstyle 11} \\ 6{,}378 \\ +\ 4{,}541 \\ \hline 10{,}919 \end{array}$$

Add the numbers in the thousands place. $6 + 4 = 10$. Regroup 10. Write the 0 in thousands place and the 1 in the ten-thousands place.

$$6{,}378 + 4{,}541 = 10{,}919$$

Adding larger numbers is easy! Just add one column at a time.

— BRING IT ON!

artial sums are used to add numbers in another way.

Look at the problem **24 + 37.**

	tens	ones
24 can be broken into	20	4
37 can be broken into	30	7

Begin by adding only the ones. There are 4 ones and 7 ones.

$$4 + 7 = 11$$

The number 11 is called a partial sum because it is a part of the whole sum.

Now add this partial sum (11) to the tens.

$$11 + 20 + 30 = 61$$

So, 24 + 37 = 61

Sums

Let's try **1,316 + 2,590.**

	thousands	hundreds	tens	ones
1,316 is broken into	1,000	300	10	6
2,590 is broken into	2,000	500	90	0

Add the ones. $6 + 0 = 6$

Add the partial
sum 6 to the tens.

$$\begin{array}{r} 6 \\ 10 \\ + 90 \\ \hline 106 \end{array}$$

Add the partial
sum 106 to the
hundreds.

$$\begin{array}{r} 106 \\ 300 \\ + 500 \\ \hline 906 \end{array}$$

Add the partial
sum 906 to the
thousands.

$$\begin{array}{r} 906 \\ 1,000 \\ + 2,000 \\ \hline 3,906 \end{array}$$

$1,316 + 2,590 = 3,906$

Rounding to

You can estimate the answer to an addition problem by rounding each number to the greatest (largest) place value.

The greatest place value of the numbers 329 and 674 is the hundreds place.

$$\begin{array}{ccc} \text{hundreds} & \text{tens} & \text{ones} \\ 3 & 2 & 9 \\ 6 & 7 & 4 \end{array}$$

When you round to the hundreds place, look at the tens place. If the digit in the tens place is 5 or greater, round up. If it is less than 5, round down.

300 | 350 400 450 500 550 600 650 | 700

329   674

329 has a 2 in the tens place. The digit 2 is less than 5, so 329 is closer to 300 than to 400. 329 rounds down to 300.

674 has a 7 in the tens place. The digit 7 is greater than 5, so 674 is closer to 700 than to 600. 674 rounds up to 700.

Estimate

Estimate 329 + 674.

329 rounds to 300.   300
674 rounds to 700.   + 700
                          1,000

The estimated sum of 329 and 674 is 1,000.

What do you do if the two numbers you are adding have different numbers of digits? Round to the greatest place value of the smaller number. Let's look at an example.

Estimate 921 + 64.

The smaller number is 64. The greatest place value of 64 is the tens place, so round both numbers to the tens place.

921 rounded to the tens place is 920.   920
 64 rounded to the tens place is 60.   + 60
                                             980

The estimated sum of 921 and 64 is 980.

Mental

You can use mental math to solve addition problems. One way to do this is to group numbers to make sets of ten.

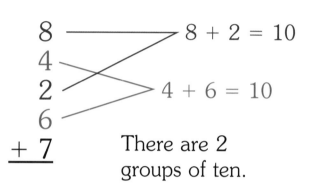

8   8 + 2 = 10
4
2   4 + 6 = 10
6
+ 7

There are 2 groups of ten.

Remember:
You can group the numbers in any order and it won't change the answer.

2 tens + 7, or 20 + 7 = 27

So, 8 + 4 + 2 + 6 + 7 = 27

Addition

You can also take from one of the numbers and give the same amount to another number without changing the final answer.

Make 32 an even ten
by taking 2 from the 32
and giving it to the 56.

$$32 + 56$$

$$- 2 \quad + 2$$

Now it is easy to
add mentally.

$$30 + 58 = 88$$

Since 32 + 56 = 30 + 58, then 32 + 56 = 88.

Adding

Coins have values in cents. The symbol ¢ means "cents." To know the total value of a number of coins, you need to add the value of all the coins.

If you have a dime, nickel, and penny, how many cents do you have in all?

dime = 10¢

nickel = 5¢

penny = 1¢

$$10¢ + 5¢ + 1¢ = 16¢$$

You have 16 cents in all.

Quarters have a value of 25¢. It is easier to add money if you memorize the value of up to four quarters.

25¢

50¢

75¢

100¢

Money

Coin values can be added quickly by counting. Count by tens for dimes, fives for nickels, and ones for pennies.

If you have 1 quarter, 2 dimes, 3 nickels, and 6 pennies, how many cents do you have in all?

Add the quarters first. One quarter is 25¢.

Now add the 2 dimes. Begin at 25¢ and count up by tens. After 25 is 35, 45. You have 45¢ so far.

Now add 3 nickels. Begin at 45 and count by fives. After 45 is 50, 55, 60. You have 60¢ so far.

Now add the 6 pennies. Begin at 60 and count by ones. After 60 is 61, 62, 63, 64, 65, 66.

You have a total of 66 cents.

Adding

To add time values, add minutes to minutes, and hours to hours.

2 hours 22 minutes + 5 hours 10 minutes

Write the problem in columns. Line up matching units.

$$\begin{array}{r} 2 \text{ hours } 22 \text{ minutes} \\ + \ 5 \text{ hours } 10 \text{ minutes} \\ \hline \end{array}$$

Add minutes first. Add just as you would any two-digit number.

$$\begin{array}{r} 2 \text{ hours } 22 \text{ minutes} \\ + \ 5 \text{ hours } 10 \text{ minutes} \\ \hline 32 \text{ minutes} \end{array}$$

Add hours. Add just as you would any one-digit number.

$$\begin{array}{r} 2 \text{ hours } 22 \text{ minutes} \\ + \ 5 \text{ hours } 10 \text{ minutes} \\ \hline 7 \text{ hours } 32 \text{ minutes} \end{array}$$

The sum of 2 hours 22 minutes + 5 hours 10 minutes is 7 hours 32 minutes.

Time

Time values can be regrouped.

2 hours 45 minutes + 8 hours 20 minutes

Add minutes first.
Since 65 minutes is
more than 1 hour, regroup.

$$\begin{array}{r} 2 \text{ hours } 45 \text{ minutes} \\ +\ 8 \text{ hours } 20 \text{ minutes} \\ \hline 65 \text{ minutes} \end{array}$$

65 minutes = 60 minutes + 5 minutes.
A group of 60 minutes can be regrouped as 1 hour.
60 minutes = 1 hour

Write 5 minutes in the
the minutes column. Carry
the 1 to the hours column.

$$\begin{array}{r} 1 \\ 2 \text{ hours } 45 \text{ minutes} \\ +\ 8 \text{ hours } 20 \text{ minutes} \\ \hline 5 \text{ minutes} \end{array}$$

Add hours.

$$\begin{array}{r} 1 \\ 2 \text{ hours } 45 \text{ minutes} \\ +\ 8 \text{ hours } 20 \text{ minutes} \\ \hline 11 \text{ hours } \ 5 \text{ minutes} \end{array}$$

The sum of 2 hours 45 minutes + 8 hours 20 minutes
is 11 hours 5 minutes.

Addition

Say you have six red shirts and five blue shirts. How many shirts do you have all together? The words "and" and "together" tell you that you should add the number of red shirts and the number of blue shirts.

6 red shirts + 5 blue shirts = 11 shirts

Words that help you know how to solve problems are called key words. Key words for addition problems are listed in the table below.

Addition Key Words		
add	combined	more than
additional	exceeds	plus
all	gain	raise
all together	greater	sum
and	in addition to	together
both	in all	total

Key Words

You can use key words to change a word problem into a math problem.

Trisha's class collected bottles for recycling. The first week they collected 21 bottles. The second week they collected 55 bottles. How many bottles did they collect all together?

The key words "all together" tell you to add the number of bottles.

21 bottles + 55 bottles = 76 bottles
Trisha's class collected 76 bottles all together.

Math problems are everywhere, but they are usually in the form of word problems. Changing word problems into math problems is a skill you use every day.

Suppose you collect model cars. You have 17 model cars at home. You find a box at a yard sale that has 9 model cars in it. How many model cars will you have in all if you buy the cars at the yard sale?

$$17 + 9 = 26$$

Problems

1 **Read** the problem carefully. Find what you know: There are 17 cars at home and 9 at the yard sale. Then find what you want to know: The total number of cars you will have if you buy the ones at the yard sale.

2 **Decide** how you can solve the problem. The key words "in all" tell you that you can add to solve the problem.

3 **Solve** the problem. Add the number of cars at home to the number of cars at the yard sale.

$$
\begin{array}{r}
\overset{1}{1}7 \\
+\ 9 \\
\hline
26
\end{array}
\begin{array}{l}
\text{cars at home} \\
\text{cars at the yard sale} \\
\text{cars in all}
\end{array}
$$

4 **Check** your work. Make sure you have answered the right question, and check your addition for mistakes.

Further Reading

Creative Teaching Press. *Addition and Subtraction Facts to 20*. Santa Barbara, Calif.: Creative Teaching Press, 2002.

Helakoski, Leslie, and Sal Murdocca. *The Smushy Bus*. Brookfield, Conn.: Millbrook Press, 2002.

Leedy, Loreen. *Mission: Addition*. New York: Holiday House, 1999.

Moore, Jo E. *Addition With Carrying*. Monterey, Calif.: Evan-Moor Educational Publishers, 1996.

Williams, Rozanne Lanczak. *The Coin Counting Book*. Watertown, Mass.: Charlesbridge Publishing, 2001.

Internet Addresses

A+ Math. "Addition Flashcards." © 1998–2004.
 <http://www.aplusmath.com/Flashcards/addition.
  html>

Gamequarium. "Addition Games."
 <http://www.gamequarium.com/addition.html>

The Math Forum. "Ask Dr. Math." © 1994–2004.
 <http://mathforum.org/library/drmath/sets/
  elem_addition.html>

Index